Jaipur was painted pink to welcome Prince Edward of Wales in 1876 since pink is the colour of hospitality. It is the first planned city of India built on the principles of Indian science of architecture, Vastu Shastra.

When they arrive, he is amazed—it's not all pink. Everyone is dressed in such bright colours! There are camels and elephants on the roads! And... so many people who are not Indians.

When they reach Sneha's house, Shivi is surprised and sad to see that Sneha is on a wheelchair. How will they play?

When he woke up next morning, he was surprised to see peacocks and monkeys outside his window!

They stop at MI Road to have kachori, lassi and jalebi. Shivi loves sweets and Jaipur has the most delicious ones!

Outside the Palace, Dadu buys an angrakha and pagdi for Shivi and a gota lehenga, borla, bindi and bangles for Sneha. Sneha teases Shivi.

At night, Shivi and Sneha try to put up a puppet show. They are not good at handling the puppets and make a big mess of it. All laugh as the puppets fall.

Try making a puppet at home. It's a fun way to tell stories.

Chokhi Dhani is so vibrant! There are ghoomar dancers, folk singers, camel rides and mouth-watering food. Because he loves the food, Shivi eats too much.

That night, Shivi has a bad stomach ache.

You know, when you eat too much, your tummy hurts. Sneha, give him some Pudinhara.

1. There were many animals like camels, elephants, peacocks and monkeys.
2. There were too many beautiful places!
3. The food was superb but I've learnt to be careful. When I eat too much, I get a stomach ache.
4. Sneha couldn't run but we had so much fun. There were special roads for her wheelchair everywhere!
5. Sneha's family was so nice to us. I must send them the photos we took.

The special road for the differently abled is called a ramp. Are there any ramps in your city for the differently abled?

What do you enjoy most on your trips?

Date: